Group Building Skills

New Hope
Birmingham, Alabama

JUDY HAMLIN

Published by:
New Hope
P. O. Box 12065
Birmingham, AL 35202-2065

Cover illustration by Cathy Robbins

Dewey Decimal classification: 266.007

Subject Headings: MISSIONS—HANDBOOKS, MATERIALS, ETC.
                  LEADERSHIP
                  GROUP RELATIONS TRAINING
                  VOLUNTEERS

Series: Leadership Skills for Women

ISBN: 1-56309-083-X

N933107•0694•7.5M1

Church Study Course number 03-351

Contents

Introduction

Congratulations! You are a leader! The title not only sounds great; it reflects the confidence others have shown in your ability to accomplish things. When you accept a leadership role, you receive at least two benefits. First, you can feel good about yourself simply because you took the risk and accepted the challenge. Second, being a leader means you have the opportunity to think and learn more, enabling you to use your new skills not only at church, but in your family, community, and workplace as well.

With these benefits, of course, come certain responsibilities. Remember, there are no leaders without followers. Those who follow you have certain needs that only you as their leader, can meet. You will be required to learn new skills, improve your expertise in some areas, and simply keep doing your best in other areas. Like it or not, you will become a role model to those who follow you. Never forget this. What you do and how you do it will be perceived by many of your followers as "the way" it should be done.

I urge you to try new approaches, to reach and teach followers both meaning and ministry through missions. As we approach a new century, a new time, you'll be faced with challenges many of us never had to deal with, and you'll often have to work with women who lack missions backgrounds and have little knowledge of what missions is all about.

Most of the examples you'll read about in this book are based on my personal experience as Women's Minister of Prestonwood Baptist Church, in Dallas, Texas. There I found that experience is the best teacher. I didn't have all the answers as I began my ministry. I prayed and sought the Lord, then learned both from my mistakes and the counsel of close friends.

I thank those friends active in missions at Prestonwood: Shirley Reynolds, Ada Hall, Mickay Minnie, Evelyn McNeill, Debbie Webb, Erma Taylor, Steve Byrd, and so many others. These women and men were the missions torch bearers at Prestonwood, and were my friends.

I dedicate this book to the memory of Bev Butler, a fine Christian role model, and an effective leader.

Now, as you move through these pages, build from your current level of understanding. Never consider your job done. Take what fits and apply or adapt it. Take your skills and everything you already know, and get going!

CHAPTER 1

Understanding the Group

Leadership in missions-oriented groups means more than showing up to host a meeting, being a project leader, or coordinating an event. It calls for leaders who will exercise both acquired and God-given skills, and who will develop practical understanding so they can effectively lead those who follow them. One of the first steps is to make sure you truly understand the dynamics of group interaction, the arena in which you will lead.

Functions of a Group

In this book, small groups are defined as people with similar interests or needs, grouped together for missions experiences. Larger, expanded groups may be similarly described, only they have broader parameters. Groups exist for a number of reasons, serve a variety of purposes, and function according to their different reasons for existence.

We will begin by looking at some of those reasons. Carl George[1] of the Charles E. Fuller Institute identifies four primary functions that take place in groups: loving, learning, doing, and deciding. Let's look closer at these functions.

• *Loving* indicates sharing, encouraging, and relating positively to one another. Whatever other purposes and functions the group has, as members learn to love and care for one another,

1

the group is strengthened.

- *Learning* includes teaching as well as studying and seeking information. Learning will probably take place at various stages of group development and involvement.
- *Doing* means putting feet on faith in a variety of ways, including missions projects and involvement. The amount of *doing* the group chooses will be determined by a number of factors, such as the interests and abilities of group members, the time allotted, and the money and leadership available.
- *Maintaining* involves the group's methods of conducting its business affairs, arranging an agenda, securing a commitment to common action, and accomplishing action items. The maintaining function takes place initially and continues as the group progresses toward goals or purposes.

Most groups formed for the purpose of missions involvement perform all of these functions to a degree. However, the majority of the group's time will be spent with the primary missions focus, and this becomes the dominant function. George uses circles to show how different groups vary in the percentage of time they spend on these four key functions.

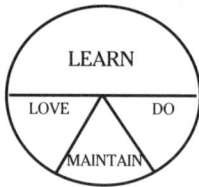

A CARING GROUP   A STUDY GROUP   A SERVING GROUP

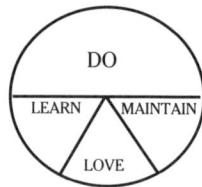

Your group may already be formed and functioning. In that case, you know the primary purpose of the group. How would you illustrate this circle to describe the group's function? One way to determine the primary and secondary functions of a group is to ask, Why was the group formed? What will be its main activity? Which functions are most important in order for the group to accomplish their purpose?

If you lead, or are involved in, other groups, how would you chart those groups' functions? On a separate sheet of paper, draw circle charts for each of these groups. How do these groups compare with one another?

2

Mechanics of a Group

What is it that really makes a group tick? The answer is group mechanics, those inner workings like communication, group involvement, and consensus on the direction of the group. All these elements involve action, participation, and cooperation among all group members. The greater the use of good group mechanics, the greater the increase in understanding, retention, involvement, and enjoyment of group members.

Read the following list of components of group mechanics to help you understand your role as group leader, improve your leadership skills, and discover ways to use these components to make your group a success.

Communication. One of the most important processes that takes place in a group is communication. In a healthy group, members actively listen to one another.

It's important to know that other people care enough to listen to what you say. Learning to listen is the most basic skill of communication. Does your mind wander when someone is talking to you? Does your expression stay the same while you're listening to someone?

To be a good communicator, you must first be a good listener. As you read these characteristics of a good listener, ask yourself if this description fits you. A good listener:
•allows others to complete their sentences without interrupting or adding words;
•does not silently contradict the speaker;
•hears what the speaker says the first time;
•gives the speaker full attention;
•does not interrupt the other person in the middle of an idea;
•is aware of other communication modes besides verbal ones;
•does not give an opinion before it is asked for;
•looks at the person who is speaking.

Communication rule number one: listen carefully when the other person is speaking. Communication rule number two: when you are the one speaking, keep in mind how easily others can miss your point. What they hear, and how they interpret what they hear, must travel through preconceived ideas, through interpretation and experience, and through other filters. Make sure you've kept your comments simple. If necessary, repeat your statement and ask for an audience response.

As the leader of the group, you have the responsibility of practicing good communication skills. You can, by your example, encourage healthy communication among group members, and make it a group characteristic. For more study on communication, read *Communication Skills* by Harriet Harral. (See the order form on the back page of this book.)

Group Involvement. Think about this statement for a moment: the leader of the group is not the group. All members of a group should be considered and involved whether the group is planning or actually performing its intended function. Let's look at three specific ways to involve the group.

• *Brainstorming* is a great way to involve group members in the decision-making process as they generate ideas through consensus and teamwork. First, gather your people, who'll have diverse backgrounds and experience, and give them a topic for discussion. Ask them to write down action ideas on the topic, with no limitations. Keep in mind the thought that no idea or suggestion is wrong.

Next, share all ideas with the group, without judging or prioritizing them. Encourage group members to begin dividing the ideas into categories such as workable, unworkable, and possibly workable. Try to have a number of suggestions that are judged either workable or possible.

Then, seriously evaluate the ideas through open discussion. Can two or more be combined? Can they be amended or changed to work better? Work with the group until they reach a consensus about which ideas should be cut, which combined, which pursued. Consider factors such as time involvement, cost, and personnel requirements.

Finally, select an appropriate number of ideas that show the greatest potential. Once the group is in agreement, ask members to help form a plan of action for implementing the idea. If additional steps need to be taken before taking action, plan to follow through. For example, you may need to coordinate your plans with other organizations, the church council, or other groups involved in similar ministries or projects.

Allow me to use a personal illustration. Our group decided to take a survey to determine whether or not our group meeting times were meeting needs within our church. Before taking the

4

survey, we held a brainstorming session on "perceived" problems in getting people to attend functions. This did not identify all the real reasons, but it did prepare leadership for what was coming in the survey. The brainstorming helped us identify many reasons that were actually given in the survey. This gave leadership authority to the group, created anticipation for the survey results, and prepared the way for change. While brainstorming new ways to meet some of the real needs identified in the survey, one of the most effective events in our ministry was born. This brainstorming exercise almost always produces effective tools for building the group, and always contributes to cohesiveness and camaraderie among members.

• *Group activities* are an important element in group involvement as the group performs its function or accomplishes its purpose. Once a group is formed, and the direction is planned, well-chosen activities will keep the group involved. An activity as used in this example may be actual, hands-on involvement or experience, or may be broadened to include activities such as studying or planning.

Think of the actions that take place within your group, those actions designed to accomplish the purpose of the meeting, as activities. Use the following guidelines to help you choose and incorporate successful activities into your meetings.

• Make sure the activity (and the meeting) starts (and ends) at the scheduled time.
• The activities planned should be enjoyable, producing an atmosphere of motivation within the group to accomplish the group's purpose.
• Directions about the activity should be clear to everyone.
• Define the amount of time the activity will take.
• The activity should be well planned and organized, moving the group from one stage to the next.
• All activities that involve the group should direct the group's focus towards their main purpose.
• The activity should include every person in the group in some way. Respect those group members who prefer not to take a visible role, but look for ways to include and involve them in the total group process.
• The activity should help group members relate to one another. All members should feel they are important to the rest of the group.

5

• Help members see how all of the group's activities are relevant to the group and to them personally.

Personal Point of View

Think about the activities on the agenda of the most recent meeting of your group.

Did you begin and end on time?

Did all group members participate?

Were members clear about the purpose or direction of the activity?

Were activities appropriate to purpose of meeting?

Did members of the group experience any changes (such as making a commitment to involvement or a change in life-style) as a result of the activity?

Direction of the Group. We have already said that groups need to have a purpose for existing, and members of the group need to know what that purpose is and what the directions are. Often, when a small group is formed, they prepare a formal covenant to guide the group. This covenant, or agreement, becomes a description of the relationship of group members to one another and to the group, and becomes a commitment of group members to one another. A covenant will help the group decide on their purpose and goals, and evaluate the results of their group functions.

Your group may choose to prepare a formal group covenant. A good starting point is to identify biblical principles and practices that apply to your group. Members might choose to include guidelines in areas such as prayer in the group; openness, affirmation, and availability of group members to one another; requirements and accountability of group members. Answering these questions will help you decide whether or not you need a formal covenant.

• How was your group formed? If the group formed around a common purpose, such as involvement in a missions project, a covenant can help you determine what responsibilities members will have to one another and to the accomplishment of the purpose. Remember, the covenant will help you set goals, determine priorities, and evaluate results.

• What is the common purpose of the group? Again, if that purpose is the accomplishment of a task, a covenant can help members find direction. A resource to help you prepare your covenant might be directions given in the leaders' material or other resources.

- What goals do group members share? A covenant can help members express their common goals, and define ways to meet those goals.
- What external factors influence the group? Is the group part of an ongoing organization in the church? If so, membership may vary according to the time of the year, membership enlistment plans, current needs, and a number of other factors. A word of caution about your group covenant: keep in mind that you do not want new members to feel excluded, or that they have to pass through some mysterious process before becoming part of the group.
- What benefits would your group have if they formed a formal covenant? Make two columns, listing reason for and against a covenant. Talk with other group members about this question and your list. Ask for their input, then ask them for their help in writing it. Avoid making it too long, binding, or restrictive. Instead of a wall to keep others out, a well-written covenant should be a band to hold members together, forming a healthy, caring group.

Perhaps your group may not feel the need for a covenant at the beginning, but as the group strengthens and the purpose becomes more clear, you find you need to clarify your objectives and goals. This can be done with a covenant or at least some type of more formal agreement.

Now, think about an example of a group. Suppose you are to create a group to complete an assigned task, such as submit a budget to the church for approval. Historically, the budget has been compiled by one person, with other members having little or no input, so members are unaware of such things as church requirements, finance limitations, and actual costs of materials and resources they will need. Awareness would make their planning more realistic.

The process of working on the budget as a group accomplishes many things. It creates a greater sense of ownership, and allows for a more complete job to be done than if one person completes the task. Specific women can be trained in particular areas, helping everyone make more informed decisions. In this case, the budgeting process becomes an excellent training ground.

This group approach also allows people with diverse backgrounds, professions, interests, and abilities to be involved together. Diversity produces sound, consensus decisions; but remember, a diverse group is more difficult to lead. Be prepared to work at the task of leadership.

If you are selecting people to work on a task group, choose both task- and relationship-oriented members. The task people will guarantee the job gets done; the relationship people will make sure decisions reflect sensitivity and compassion.

A group formed to work on a specific task should be small, preferably seven members. Fewer than five members doesn't provide enough resources to draw on. Four or six can lead to divided votes. More than seven makes it difficult for everyone to contribute. The agenda for the meeting of this group is short, giving everyone an opportunity to contribute, and to listen to one another. A good meeting will consider a few key issues in depth, leaving inconsequential items to be handled by the leader, and some items to be dealt with by the larger group.

The First Meeting of a Group

Perhaps your group is already formed. If so, think about that group as you read this section, then answer the reflection questions on page 10. If you are about to begin a group, or plan to begin a group at some time in the future, pay special attention to these *decision* steps. The important dynamic of what occurs in the first meeting will help members discover what they hope to accomplish and steps they will take to meet their goals. Let's look at some of the details that can make that first *decision* meeting successful.

• *Begin with prayer.* Ask God's guidance for the members of the group, for you as their leader, and in the work the group hopes to accomplish.

• *Set an agenda for this meeting.* Write agenda items on a blackboard or flip chart. Better yet, distribute a printed agenda ahead of time. To get the session started, state what you feel are the purpose and goals for the group, then ask members to share their ideas. Since it's vital that members agree on the goals and objectives, make sure you hear everyone's comments. Remember, always involve group members in all decisions, and move forward with changes when it's apparent that

8

they are supported by a majority. Then, when you sense a consensus or agreement, ask members to vote or voice their approval, whichever is appropriate.

Another agenda item should be the scheduling of future meeting times. Make sure your meetings will be held frequently enough to maintain continuity and interest. You may plan to meet weekly, bi-monthly, or monthly. Determine the length of meetings; allow enough time for covering priority action items and for fellowship.

- *Make allowances for differences.* Some in your group will be anxious to make decisions, and have definite ideas about directions for the group being formed. For some group members, making a decision produces anxiety. They always want more information. For others, anxiety is created by what appears to be "endless rehashing" of a subject. Rather than more information, they want action.

- *Keep expectations reasonable.* Only so much can be accomplished in this meeting. As a leader, you have provided structure and encouragement for presenting and exploring ideas, not finding all the perfect solutions. You will need to look at discussions from two vantage points: what is ideal and what is reality. The group may have plans that you as the leader recognize as beyond time and/or budget restrictions.

- *End on time.* At the appropriate time, stop the discussion and summarize the options. If members act as though they want to continue the discussion, poll them to see if they want to stay longer. If there is no consensus, you must assume responsibility for deciding whether to continue or schedule another meeting. If you decide to continue, always provide a graceful exit for those who need to leave. At the end of the meeting, thank everyone for coming, announce the next meeting date, and close with prayer.

Evaluating the First Meeting
Use the checklist on the following page to evaluate your first group meeting.

YES NO
___ ___ Started on time
___ ___ Ended on time

___ ___ Atmosphere was non-threatening
___ ___ Discussion allowed everyone to participate
___ ___ Group purpose and goals were agreed upon
___ ___ All points of view were encouraged
___ ___ Questions of judgement were decided by the group
___ ___ Agenda items were brief and clear
___ ___ The proceedings were orderly
___ ___ Unclear statements were clarified
___ ___ Creative thinking resulted
___ ___ Decisions were made, and a plan formulated

Personal Point of View

At the beginning of this section, we mentioned the possibility that your group may already be established. If that is the case, take time now to evaluate your leadership role, and the group's goals and directions.

Have you taken the steps described above?

Is the group clear about its purpose and direction?

Do you need to stop now and reestablish the direction and purpose of the group?

A final note: meetings may not be a requirement for your group. For example, if the purpose of the group is to perform a specific task, the group may be involved in action that is done outside of a meeting. Most of the same guidelines are true for this group as they are for all groups. In fact, members may need to work at developing a group bond.

[1]For further information on this Love-Learn-Do-Maintain concept, see *The Coming Church Revolution: Empowering Leaders for the Future* by Carl F. George with Warren Bird (Grand Rapids, Mich.: Fleming H. Revell, 1994), chapter 18. For further information, contact 1-800-627-6382.

CHAPTER 2

Leading the Group

I've read books on leadership, led leadership training, taught characteristics of an effective leader, but to me, effective leadership boils down to two basic qualities: compassion (agape love) and encouragement. People are looking for leaders who will pray for them and for a place to belong, to be significant and accepted. Under your leadership, your group can meet these needs.

Be an Encourager

Jesus modeled encouragement for His followers. He changed Simon's name to Peter, which means rock, though Simon considered himself a sinful man (John 1:40-42). Jesus referred to Nathanael as "a true Israelite, in whom there is nothing false" (John 1:47-51). He called Zacchaeus "son of Abraham," and said He would like to stay at Zacchaeus' house (Luke 19:1-10). The Bible describes how Zachaeus' behavior changed after that dinner. The Pharisees saw a sinful woman who washed Jesus' feet with her tears and perfume and then dried them with her hair. But Jesus forgave her sins and saw the beauty of her actions (Luke 7:36-47).

Do you bring out the best in others? That's perhaps the single most important trait of leadership. As the leader of a group,

11

your skills can be enhanced as you learn and practice these principles of encouragement. Alan Loy McGinnis[1] suggests that there are some universal principles that help us do this:

- Have high quality and achievement standards. Communicate these to others, then stick to them.
- Use specifics to compliment and encourage others. Rather than "You did a good job leading the meeting," say "That was great the way you expressed appreciation to Tony during the meeting today."
- Affirm the good things about others. Not only does this help the one affirmed; it also encourages others. Publicly acknowledge these good things.
- Point out scriptural heroes such as Abraham and Moses— people whom the Bible records as having done something extraordinary. Reflecting on the heroes of our faith somehow challenges us to be better followers of Christ.
- Be sincere. People know whether or not you are sincere. If they question your motives in this area, they will question them in other areas as well.

Can you be the person who will help someone else do better what they already know they can do? If so, you're a leader.

Personal Point of View

Write the names of three people in your group.

Now beside those names, write a statement of affirmation. Look for natural opportunities to verbalize these affirmations.

Be Decisive

Leadership calls for decision making free from the unnecessary fear of failure. As the leader of a group, opportunities for decisiveness come many times and in many forms. The knowledge that you will surely make mistakes must not paralyze you so that you do not make decisions at all. When wrong decisions are made, the decisive leader analyzes the problem then looks for a workable solution.

Again I will use a personal example. One of our major churchwide missions involvement events was our "Back-to-School" dinner and clothing distribution for economically disadvantaged children. While planning the third annual program, a major hurdle appeared. The event had always been held on the third floor of the church, a space which at best would only accommodate 250 people. It became obvious that we were going to attract close to 500 people.

While I was away at a staff retreat, the group in charge decided to leave the event on the third floor and not move it to our Fellowship Hall, which could easily handle the increased numbers. Someone called to inform me.

The group had acted decisively, but had made what I felt was the wrong decision. At first I was angry, but I then reasoned out why they would make such a decision. The event was scheduled for Thursday evening, following the regular Wednesday night dinner, which meant that the set-up of thousands of pieces of clothing would have to be accomplished in one day by a group of volunteers with one slow elevator and two carts.

Reflecting on our goal for this event, I knew that staying on the third floor was not the right decision. When I returned from the staff retreat I met with the group leaders and together we posed and answered a few questions.

• What have been our main problems the last two years? Answer: too little space for the event; not ending soon enough for the Bus Ministry to return everyone to their homes at a reasonable hour.

• Why leave the event on the third floor? Answer: because of lack of time and manpower involved in moving the clothing.

• Why would it be better to have it in Fellowship Hall? Answer: to have more room.

• How could we make the move quickly and efficiently? Do we have a church member who has connections with a moving company? After investigation, we learned that we did.

Solution: Early Thursday morning, the church member who owned a moving company appeared with his crew and transported all the clothing to Fellowship Hall before noon.

Results: We had a very successful event as well as a good model for identifying and overcoming obstacles. The situation became a demonstration of respect for leadership and success through teamwork, while at the same time maintaining a decisive attitude. Also, our guests and Bus Ministry team returned home at a reasonable hour. By prayerfully making decisions, God helped us solve our problems, and move the event to a better location. Ultimately, the event glorified Him.

Personal Point of View

Is there a decision you need to make?

What decisive steps do you need to take?

Share Leadership

Sharing leadership is not optional, it's mandatory for accomplishing a mission. In fact, there's one central problem in groups I've observed over the years—a lack of shared leadership. One way I demonstrate this principle is to take a plate of cookies to a table of five people and offer a cookie to one, two, three, or four individuals but never all five. Then after walking away, I ask those who didn't get a cookie how they feel. Responses vary from "left out" and "awkward" to "why me?" Of course, once my point has been made, I give cookies to those who were omitted the first time.

Shared leadership will help a group reach its goals, cut the time it takes to reach them, make the journey more fun, distribute the strength it takes to accomplish goals, and help others feel needed and wanted. Scripture offers many examples and patterns of shared leadership, such as King David who raised an army to protect a nation; Gideon and his 300 hand picked soldiers; Noah and his sons who built the ark; Paul, who worked with and through many Christians.

Failure to delegate limits the leader's capacities. Moses learned this lesson. Even with his God-given abilities, he needed the help of others (Ex. 18:20). Lack of shared leadership is the number one problem causing burnout in leaders. I've tried "going it alone" on major projects, and yes, I've burned out. However, on projects in which I've empowered others to help carry out the goals and dreams, not only did I not burn out—it seemed that before the project was completed, God was giving me another vision. Putting it another way, "What sound does the band make when there's only a band leader?"

Remember my Back-to-School event? Evelyn volunteered to organize the clothing for the event, so she was willing. But was she able? For sure, since she had previously owned and operated her own thrift store. Suggestions from me would have only hampered her part of the task.

14

Mickay volunteered to head up the Mission Fair, an annual event that required booths in the church atrium during Sunday services. They were decorated and manned to inform the entire church body of missions service opportunities. This was a massive undertaking, but Mickay had been in mission work for years, led groups, and worked in every church department. She is a personal friend and I knew she would ask for help if she needed it. I was also confident the event would be the best ever—and it was. I specifically recall one church member's comment: "This is the most effective display we have ever had in the church atrium." Mickay always worked effectively through others, and that way she built up a following of people she used on other projects.

The Evelyns and Mickays are more talented and motivated than the norm. You need people like them because they provide a foundation for expansion of your ministry, and free up time for coaching or supporting other volunteers.

Not all situations turn out positively. Alice accepted responsibility for decorations. She had held the position before and thoroughly enjoyed her work, but she had recently taken a part-time job. I assumed she could do the job by seeking any coaching and support she needed. Well, she didn't need coaching but did need support. Because of her part-time job she often left early, missing fellowship with the other women, and the support and appreciation of others. She made it through half the year, then burned out and quit.

Personal Point of View

What is your vision for your group?

How can you share this vision with others in the group?

How can sharing leadership help your group achieve its goals?

Share Your Vision

Shared vision is a leader's ability to discern a path for the future and convey that vision to others. Conveying the vision is paramount to success of the group. How then, do we convey our dreams and goals?

Focusing on God's vision, lead the group to compose a mission statement that short enough for people to remember and specific enough to describe what you are trying to accomplish. When people who are not involved ask questions about the group's purpose and missions work, those in the group can quickly and confidently recite or explain the mission statement with excitement. Involve everyone in creating a plan to carry out missions. When a goal has been achieved, publicly acknowledge the people involved and stress the importance of the ministry if it will be continued.

Practice Good Leadership Skills

When leading a group meeting, it is important to give each member the opportunity to state opinions, make contributions, and feel they are a part of the group. As the leader, you have the responsibility of keeping the group expectations balanced. If the primary function of your group is *doing* (see chapter 1), members will expect to make decisions, plan, and serve—but not spend much time on sharing and other relational activities. If *caring* or *learning* is the primary function of your group, members will expect little business to be conducted but welcome sharing and relationship-building time, or time to study.

Jesus modeled group-leading skills for us as He led His band of disciples. He equipped them to carry on His mission by guiding them as they travelled together, worked together, and learned together. Leading a group calls for your best in leadership skills. Discover them; develop them; improve them; then use them for His glory.

Personal Point of View

As you review this chapter, think of Biblical examples of ways Jesus:
•was an encourager.
•was decisive.
•shared leadership.
•shared His vision.
•demonstrated good leadership skills.

---

[1]Adapted from McGinnis, Alan Loy, *The Friendship Factor*, Baptist Spanish Publishing House, El Paso, Texas, 1982.

CHAPTER 3

Understanding the Group Leader

One of the most important single elements in assuring the success of small group interaction is to match leadership style with the make up of group members. The first step in making this match is to understand different leadership styles and how they relate to group participants.

There are many terms used to describe leadership styles. Roberta Hestenes[1] uses the terms *autocratic, authoritative, democratic,* and *laissez-faire*. Read her descriptions of these styles in the following chart:

Leadership Styles

Autocratic (Domineering, dictatorial)
1. Total control, with members as listeners and followers.
2. Determines goals and policies.
3. More interested in subject matter (content) than people (process).
4. Makes decisions regardless of other views.
5. Talks too much.
6. Focuses attention on himself or herself.
7. Group members are almost puppets.
8. Asks and answers all questions.

17

Authoritative (Definite yet responsive)
1. Strong control, with members actively involved in the discussions.
2. Has a definite purpose and plan but is open to modification.
3. Active and energetic and seeks the activity of others.
4. Prepared to give direction and support as needed.
5. Uses communication skills to involve others.
6. Takes responsibility until others can assume it.
7. Uses personal power to empower others.
8. Prepares and asks questions; members respond.

Democratic (Group-centered)
1. Shared control, with leader and members sharing functions.
2. Shares leadership responsibility.
3. Believes in other people.
4. Creates a sense of security and belonging.
5. Ensures that others have chance to lead.
6. If leader withdraws, group will not fall apart.
7. Sees that group discusses all policies.
8. May ask others to lead discussion, using guide.

Laissez-faire (Permissive, passive)
1. Minimal control, with members directing.
2. Doesn't prepare and lets things drift.
3. Doesn't seem to care.
4. Causes the group to accomplish very little.
5. Encourages fragmentation through lack of discipline.
6. Makes no attempt to appraise or regulate events.
7. Lacks courage in making decisive plans.
8. Asks one vague or general question, then is silent.

Personal Point of View

Read these leadership style descriptions again. This time identify three of your leadership weaknesses. Recall a time when you encountered each of these weaknesses. Think about the response of group members on those occasions. What could you have done differently in each situation?

What can you do to avoid this happening in the future?

Now list three of your leadership strengths. Can you develop these strengths even more?

How do your group members respond to these strengths?

Case Studies

Below are some problem scenarios, followed by suggested solutions. After reading the case study, think about a plan of action you might take in this situation. Then read the suggested solution that follows. These examples can become guides to help you recognize situations with which you must deal, and consider plans of action.

• A member begins talking about information that is not on the day's agenda.

Did the group have a copy of the agenda, or was the agenda in your mind only? If you did not have a printed agenda, this is the first step to take in dealing with the problem. The leader should model the desired behavior, organization, commitment to the project, and attention to detail. If you have emphasized the importance of following an agenda from the start, it will be easier to move the discussion back on track.

• Outside interruptions disturb your group meeting.

Create a plan to deal with outside interruptions. Appoint someone in the group to be responsible in case someone comes to the door of your meeting room. Post signs stating that a meeting is in progress; include the ending time. If you're meeting in a home, have someone designated to answer the telephone or doorbell.

• A group member's behavior disrupts the group meeting.

If a group member continually interrupts discussions, perhaps you should meet with that person before or after the meeting to discuss any personal problems that you may not be aware of. Again, it may be helpful to assign time limits on each agenda item. Discovering the root of the behavior problem is the first step to take, then prayerfully confront the problem.

• Group members want to "chase rabbits."

If you experience repeated attempts by members to get off the subject, reevaluate the project or purpose of the group by asking yourself these questions: *Did all group members partici-pate in setting the goals of the group? Is the desired outcome do-able? Is it valuable? Do all members have enough information to carry out their parts of the project? Have you delegated enough responsibility to members?*

If the answer is no to any of these questions, these actions might be helpful: equally distribute tasks among the group while retaining your role as leader. Call a meeting for the pur-pose of clarification of the project. Remind members of the orig-inal purpose of the group; in a non-threatening way, ask each to recommit to the project and group. Follow this up with a time of prayer.

If your answers to the questions above are yes, use well-planned discussion questions to bring the group back to the project at hand.

• The group doesn't have enough time for meetings.

Reconsider the size of your group. Is it small enough for everyone to be able to participate in discussions? If the size is right, is enough time being spent on prayer and sharing before getting to the task at hand? If a group is comfortable in their relationships with each other, the task actually goes faster.

• Members are disagreeable and seem to be uncooperative. Realize there are stages in a group's development. See page 24 for a more detailed discussion of group development.

• Group members have blank looks on their faces and no one speaks or asks questions.

Perhaps members don't know enough to ask questions, and you should provide more information. Taking time to give back-ground information on a particular ministry, event, mission pro-ject, or Bible study will almost always result in a clearer under-standing, thus facilitating future discussion. Be clear and con-cise, provide written materials, use visuals, and make all of your contributions pertinent.

Personal Point of View

Now it's your turn. Hopefully, the following questions will help you in making observations on group behavior and finding creative solutions to difficult situations that have a tendency to keep us off track. After you have thought of your own solutions, read my suggestions on page 52.

What would you do if . . .
- more than half the group members are late?
- two group members are carrying on a private conversation during the meeting?
- members cannot come to a consensus?
- you don't have enough time to complete the priority items on your agenda?
- you observe leadership qualities in a group member?
- a member frequently misses meetings?
- two or more members begin to argue?
- you are having a bad day and it's time for your meeting?

Remember that learning to lead is a process, developed through constant reading, study, and application. Devote some time each day to building your leadership skills. You might choose to do this by:
- studying all the books in the *Leadership Skills for Women* series (see the order form on the back page of this book). After studying all six books and completing the requirements, you can receive a *Leadership Skills for Women in Missions* diploma (see p. 56).
- asking your church media center director for leadership skills books that are available or could be ordered.
- looking for other leadership resources at your local Christian bookstore.
- taking advantage of leadership classes offered in your church or community.

[1]Adapted from Hestenses, Roberta, *Using the Bible in Groups.* © 1983 Roberta Hestenes. Used by permission of Westminster/John Knox Press.

CHAPTER 4

Understanding the Members of the Group

An effective group draws on all members to achieve a goal that cannot be reached by one person. Consider a football team, made up of eleven people who must advance against another team of eleven. Team resources include a quarterback, receivers, runners, and linemen; it cannot succeed without everyone running planned plays in unison. However, even running plays in unison doesn't guarantee success. The same is true with a group, whether it's a committee, a charitable organization, or a group working on a missions project.

Personality Types

Groups are made up of all sorts of people who have very different personality types. Psychologists group personalities into four basic categories; Florence Littauer[1] adds these descriptive words that can help us understand these classifications: Sanguine/Popular; Choleric/Powerful; Melancholy/Perfect; and Phlegmatic/Peaceful. We can avoid possible conflicts when we understand why people act and react as they do. By knowing others' strengths and weaknesses, we can better encourage and build them up, thus fulfilling our leadership role.

In *Welcome to Your First Small Group*,[2] I described how these four personality types might work together to plan a fellowship dinner. Suzy Sanguine, who is popular, outgoing, talkative, and

23

unpredictable is the chairperson. Since she realizes she is undisciplined, she enlists Karen Choleric to use her planning and organizing skills to enhance the team. For decorations, Marie Melancholy lends her perfectionist's touch, and Patsy Phlegmatic takes charge on the day of the event, taking care of all the last minute details. Do you see how each personality type contributes to the group?

I will never forget leaving a Christmas Missionary Dinner with the chairperson. The event went very well indeed but in my Choleric mode (can't relax, little tolerance for mistakes, and can do everything better), I proceeded to tell her how I thought we could improve the event the next year. Big mistake!

There is danger in becoming more interested in the subject, program or event than in people. Don't lose the personal touch. I violated this principle. Virginia, a Choleric/Melancholy who is deep and thoughtful, was quick to point out, "Judy, I would like to reflect and enjoy today. Could we talk about this later?" That hurt, and was a hard lesson for me, but now I am more observant and discerning before speaking my mind.

Spiritual Gifts of Members

Identification of spiritual gifts is also necessary when helping others find their place in ministry. Understand that discovery of spiritual gifts does not equate either to understanding or effective use. People need to know how a spiritual gift relates to their life, to others, to their church, and to the Lord's will for them. Study the New Testament to find descriptions of spiritual gifts, then think of your group members. Books such as *Uniquely Gifted* by Stuart Calvert can help you understand gifts from the Biblical perspective, and then realize ways God uses gifted people in His church today.

Stages of Development

Group members will have stages of development. First there will be a time of orientation as members get to know and understand one another and become comfortable with their own roles. Then a tougher period of negotiation will begin defining member's roles, agendas, and methods of reaching agreement. Effective leadership is particularly important here, for the leader must guide seeming conflict so that it continues to produce positive results. You must delegate responsibilities, maintaining the kind of balance that will keep diverse people enthusiastic. Finally, if everything has been done well, consensus or unity will develop, and the right decisions will result.

Groups naturally go through stages of development. While these stages vary from group to group, some form of developmental process often takes place. Students of group psychology described these stages with various titles. Kevin Thompson[3] calls them "dependence, resistance to freedom, adolescent rebellion, celebration, and independence/interdependence."

Using Thompson's explanations, these stages might be described as:

- the first stage when members look to the leader for help and direction. The leader is not certain about how much freedom to give members.
- a second stage when the leader begins to prepare members to accept more responsibility, and members tend to resist or be anxious about this responsibility.
- the third stage, compared to a rebellious teenager, when members try to gain independence and recognition. They often reject the leader, and ignore or contradict the leaders's suggestions. At this stage the leader needs the maturity necessary to accept these attitudes and avoid a power struggle.
- a fourth stage when members gain confidence in themselves, and celebrate by enjoying the group and ignoring the leader. The wise leader will recognize this stage and allow the group to develop and grow.
- a final, productive stage. Now members accept the leader and are ready to move forward as a productive team. In this stage shared leadership begins to take shape, and often the leader is able to allow the group to move forward on their own.

A group will be united and strong only if all of its members show concern for one another. All members should participate, either by providing information, making sure information is understood, bringing additional insight, or identifying points to help bring the discussion to a decision. All suggestions should be considered, and disagreements worked out to the satisfaction of the group as well as the satisfaction of the individuals having different opinions.

Some members will help keep the discussion on course, while others may want to "chase rabbits." A healthy, well-functioning group is one in which the members work together by giving, taking, and blending ideas into workable plans and solutions.

Personal Point of View

Make a list of the members of your group, identifying each one's personality type.

What unique contribution does this person make to the group because of the personality type?

What spiritual gifts does each member have?

How can you as the leader of the group encourage all members to use their gifts?

[1]Littauer, Florence. *Your Personality Tree.* Irving, Texas: Word, Inc., 1988. Video.

[2]Adapted from Hamlin, Judy, *Welcome to Your First Small Group*, Victor Books, 1993, p. 28.

[3]Adapted from Thompson, Kevin M., *Equipping the Saints: A Manual for Small Group Ministry*, Minneapolis, Minnesota, 1980.

CHAPTER 5

Identifying a Healthy Group

It goes without saying that all groups are different. They have different goals, different agendas, different purposes, and are made up of different people. It should also be obvious that some groups are healthy and some unhealthy, but often we overlook or ignore that fact. If we are aware that a group is unhealthy, we are not sure what to do about the situation, or we avoid dealing with it. This chapter defines and compares healthy and unhealthy groups, and gives you tools for identifying and improving the unhealthy ones.

Group Identity

Members of a healthy group have a feeling of belonging. They enjoy being with one another, and look forward to their times together. They make an effort to attend all meetings.

I recall one mission event that required a full day of preparation. Members agreed to work in shifts to get everything together. Some young mothers with small children had to leave when their shifts were up; however, others worked overtime to complete the project. One observer was so overwhelmed with the teamwork that she pitched in to help. The cohesiveness was obvious to even a casual observer.

27

Members of the healthy group feel pride in the group. They refer to "my" group rather than "their" group, or some other identity. How does this happen? The leader, and all members working together, encourage it by including members in decisions, plans, and activities. If a leader or member dominates the group, members will feel less ownership.

A feeling of group unity does not mean that there is no conflict. Remember the Back-to-School event when I was overruled on moving the clothing from one location to the other? The group members didn't hesitate to speak their minds because it was their backs that would suffer! Thanks to everyone's openness we sat down, discussed the issues, and found a solution. If we had not had group unity, we would have been afraid the conflict would destroy the group.

Conflict Management

As a leader, you must be prepared to handle conflict when it does occur. To be human is to be tempted by self-centeredness, disloyalty, anger, and misunderstandings. To be involved with other people means there will be a certain amount of conflict. Keep in mind that not all conflict is bad. Disagreements allow people to express their feelings, and being heard by our peers can elevate our self-esteem.

Good conflict is not so difficult to deal with. It's when conflict becomes disruptive and destructive that it becomes difficult. In a previous book,[1] I list seven steps for dealing with conflict. When conflict does occur, taking these steps can help you deal with it.

- Confront conflict when it is small, before it grows into something larger.
- Try to deal with issues involved, not with personalities.
- Recognize the feelings and concerns that others have in the situation.
- Focus on facts of the situation instead of rumors or opinions.
- Maintain a trusting and friendly attitude with all those involved.
- Clarify whether one or several issues must be dealt with, and deal with one issue at a time.
- Assemble all parties in the conflict at one meeting, and reason with all of them at the same time. As always, pray prior to the meeting. Often, if there is prayer prior to such a confronta-

tion, it will not turn into gossip or a judgment session.

I learned the hard way to confront conflict when it is still small. A Bible study group and their leader were experiencing some conflict, but all those involved wanted to avoid dealing with the issues. Then some church staff members became uncomfortable with the leader of the group. Personal attitudes, lack of prayer, pride, and the fact that the issue had not been addressed when it was small all helped create a much larger problem. At last, we called a meeting with all parties involved and discussed issues, not personalities. We looked at alternative policy opportunities and temporarily resolved the issue. However, one of the parties in the conflict later resigned. For more study on conflict, read *Conflict Management* by Shirley Schooley. (See the order form on the back page of this book.)

Other Characteristics

Healthy groups don't just happen. Some are naturally healthier than others, but like the physical body, a group needs proper nourishment and exercise to maintain its health. As you read these characteristics of healthy groups, you will notice that many are closely related.

- *Proper movitation.* Why are people involved in your group? In the healthy group, members participate because their needs are being met, and they are helping meet the needs of the group. Those who participate in daily worship, witnessing, and giving have a higher quality of motivation. Sustained motivation requires that people know what is expected of them, and usually occurs when members have the opportunity to participate in planning and decision making.
- *Wise use of members' gifts.* Forget the myth, "give a person a job and he will become active." Recognize that a person's spiritual gifts, needs, and desires should conform with God's will for them. Within the healthy group all members use the gifts they have been given, and none are called on to use gifts they do not have.
- *Respect for the individual.* Church leaders should be people-centered in their approach to the selection and enlistment of group members. People are more important than numbers, methods, or programs. People who were enlisted because they are important as individuals will form healthy groups. Praise, recognition, and appreciation should be given when

they are merited.

- *Accountability.* Members of a healthy group feel accountable to one another, and to the group as a whole. This accountability will affect the way members funtion in the group, and the way they relate to one another.
- *Balance of leader/member involvement.* Members of a healthy group share with the leader in the responsibilities and privileges of group involvement. The leader of a healthy group does not do all the leading; members feel responsible to carry their share of the load. This means that the leader delegates some of the tasks, both the pleasant and not-so-pleasant ones.
- *Communication.* Two-way communication takes place as information is shared from the leader to the group, and vice versa. Members aren't left "out in the dark," wondering what is going on. On the other hand, members do not exclude the leader from the chain of communication.
- *Attitude of teamwork.* Leaders should emphasize teamwork rather than competition, as a group incentive. "One for all and all for one" might be the motto of a healthy group.
- *Shared goals.* The importance of common goals for a group was dealt with in earlier chapters, but it is listed again here. A healthy group is certainly one that is unified in purpose.
- *Constructive handling of conflict.* This, too, was discussed earlier. Not all conflict comes in the form of verbal disagreements. Some degree of ongoing conflict usually exists as different personalities try to blend. The way the group deals with these personality conflicts is a determining factor in the group's health.

Personal Point of View

Draw two columns on a sheet of paper. As you review this chapter, list the healthy and unhealthy characteristics of a group. Then think about your own group as you review your lists. Place a check beside those entries that describe your group. Are there unhealthy characteristics you need to work to improve? Are there plans you can make for strengthening the healthy characteristics?

[1]Adapted from Hamlin, Judy, *The Small Group Leaders Training Course Leader's Manual,* NavPress, Colorado Springs, Colorado, 1990, p. 114.

CHAPTER 6

Avoiding Pitfalls

Groups, like people, are not perfect, and will never be perfect. After all, they are made up of imperfect members, and have an imperfect leader. There are, however, some common pitfalls in group dynamics that can be avoided, or at least dealt with when they do occur. Group leaders need to be aware of potential problems that can come from within the group as well as from outside sources. By learning skills that will help in solving these problems, the leader can guide members to become a healthy, functioning group. Obviously, the leader sets the tone for most participant behavior. To become a more effective leader, you must be able to quickly recognize pitfalls then be ready to react or respond to them.

A fundamental reason for the majority of our problems is ineffective communication, both with one another and with God. We should always be mindful of the instructions of Proverbs 19:21 (NASB), "Many are the plans in a man's heart, but it is the Lord's will that prevails." Isaiah put it this way: "And your ears will hear a word behind you, 'This is the way, walk in it,' whenever you turn to the right or to the left" (Isa. 30:21 NASB). Prayer is our communication with God; make it a daily part of your leadership preparation.

Some Common Pitfalls

Problems, or pitfalls, for groups usually appear in four basic areas: 1. problems related to the basics of the meetings of the group; 2. problems with leadership skills; 3. faulty administrative functions; 4. poor participant behaviors.

Below are some elements that can, and often do, cause problems for a group. As you read the list, write the number of the problem area suggested above that you feel is appropriate for each statement. For example, a group that is too large has the potential of problems in all four areas: there is a problem with the meeting; leadership needs to deal with the problem; administrative actions could relieve the problem; participant behavior is affected.

Group is too large.
Group is too small.
Location of meetings is inconvenient.
Seating arrangement is inappropriate.
Physical setting is too large, cold, or formal.
Start and stop times aren't followed.
Meeting time is too early or late.
Meeting is too long or short.
Meeting frequency is inappropriate.
There is a lack of planning.
There are unresolved conflicts.
Leader is authoritative.
Members are not encouraged.
Leader is not encouraged.
Leader does not have a vision.
Group is unclear about the purpose.
Leader is frequently absent.
Leader is often unprepared.
There is undue focus on absent members.
Participants are put on the spot.
Tense moments are ignored.
There is a lack of shared leadership.
Leader is inflexible.
There is a lack of follow-up.
Leader is not available before and after the meeting.
There is a lack of emphasis on application.
Members are not included in decision making.

Lack of transparency or openness during discussions.
Members do not realize their value to the group.
Members do not know one another.
There is a lack of prayer time.
Expectations are unclear.
Tasks are viewed as more important than participants.
Group time is not used wisely.
Meetings are often canceled.
The agenda is unclear.
Members have child care problems.
The group has no common purpose.
There is no group evaluation.
Name tags are not provided if needed.
No plan to handle interruptions.
There is a lack of participant diversity.
Members are shy or dominating.
Motives of leader and group members are faulty.
Spiritual smugness exists among some members.
Members betray confidences.
The meeting has become a social event.
Members have repeated tardiness or absenteeism.
Members have negative attitudes.
Members are critical of one another.
Cliques exist.
Personality clashes are disruptive.
There is poor interaction.
There is apathy.

Avoiding Pitfalls

How, then, can we avoid these pitfalls? You have already taken a first step by identifying them. Being aware of problems, or potential ones, gives the leader an edge. Evaluate each situation and each problem. Ask yourself, *What could I do differently to solve this problem? How can I lead members to find a workable solution? How can members help me avoid this pitfall?*

Personal Point of View

Review the list above, this time making a check on the left of the statements that are problems, or potential problems, for your group. Think about these statements. What positive steps can you take to change the situation? For example, if the meeting location is inconvenient, where could you relocate?

If members do not know one another, would using "get acquainted" questions at the beginning of meetings help?

Would more fellowship time apart from meeting time be helpful to group members?

Make notes for future reference or study as you consider these steps.

CHAPTER 7

Evaluation and Progress

One of the most valuable exercises for the long term health and effectiveness of your group is *evaluation*. Often overlooked, this step seems to have nothing to do with how you lead a group, the group's purpose, or the characteristics of your group. However, it's the key to eliminating mistakes, improving effectiveness, and reaching goals. Whether formal or informal, it must be done before, during, and after every activity.

Why Evaluate

Some of the goals of an evaluation are to discover the need for and make changes; assess the group's progress; gather facts and information; assess success of the leadership; encourage members as they progress toward their goals; and improve the ministries of the group. To move forward the group must review regularly, plans for development must be made, means to implement the plans must be provided, and progress must be checked. By your personal role in the group you can directly and effectively help the group do its work.

Evaluation of groups must be deliberate and planned, and should be used to obtain information that will help you make course corrections and group decisions. Information gained in your evaluation can provide guidance for long-range planning, so it is important that you keep good records. For best results, use the same evaluation format at several points in time, to help you formulate conclusions and observe progress.

When to Evaluate

When should evaluation take place? It should be an on-going process, but specific times should be set aside for reporting and updating. Evaluations might be made by members following regular meetings if members understand their importance. Evaluation might take place during a regular meeting, which gives members time to complete the task without it seeming like an added responsibility. Evaluation almost always improves performance, and there are a variety of methods such as observations, group evaluation activities, and questionnaires. Times for evaluation should be planned prior to beginning a group, so it can be implemented without participants feeling threatened.

If several group leaders want to evaluate their groups, or a group wants to meet together to evaluate their direction, accomplishments, or purpose, an ideal time would be during a weekend retreat, with one full day for evaluation and another for brainstorming and planning.

How to Evaluate

What should be included in an evaluation? These suggestions will help you develop your own.
• How clearly defined are the group's goals?
• Do members and leaders agree on major and minor goals?
• Do members and leaders agree on the way these goals will be reached?
• How would you rate the group's support of activities?
• Do the group's activities lead to accomplishment of the tasks?
• Do group members have the necessary resources to achieve their purpose?
• How well do members communicate with one another?
• How well do members and leader communicate?
• How would you rate your own leadership of the group?
• Do members share in the decision-making process?

This list is only a suggestion of areas you may want to include in your own evaluation form. Your group is unique. The best evaluation for your group is one that will recognize that uniqueness, and will describe your specific group's strengths and weaknesses in obtaining its goals.

Who should be involved in evaluation? Each member should participate, with the understanding that the group share all observations. In fact, the most effective evaluation takes place as the group interacts and shares their comments. This also gives the leader a chance to reflect on her leadership style.

Some members may object to evaluations, saying they are too worldly and a waste of time. Some may be afraid of negative results, and others anxious about the process. You can help your members work through their fears and objections by pointing out the benefits.

Of course, some informal evaluation will take place whether or not you plan it. Too often, it consists of one or two people sharing their frustrations or grievances after a meeting, and the group cannot profit from these private judgments. Only when critical or reflective comments are heard by the whole body can something be done about them. On the other hand, some informal evaluation takes place in the positive feedback you get, in the compliments given, in visible evidences of a healthy group. While you can't depend too strongly on these informal evaluations, they can help you discover areas where you need to do more formal evaluating.

Evaluations

Following are examples of several evaluations. The first two evaluations are for the leader only. You may want to adapt these to meet your needs, or you may choose to use another form. Questions such as these will help you evaluate your first two meetings.

Meeting One
Did everyone attend?
Did relationships get off to a good start?
Did you observe any potential problem relationships?
Did any person seem to monopolize the discussion?
Did anyone seem unusually hesitant to participate?
Were prayer requests shared and did you write them down?
Did the group agree on goals and objectives?
Did you feel comfortable in your role as leader?

After evaluating the first meeting, decide on any changes that should be made before the second meeting.

Meeting Two
Did everyone attend?
Did anyone drop out?
Do members in the group appear to be bonding?
Did everyone contribute to the discussion?
Did you follow-up on last week's prayer requests?
Is the group moving toward its goals?
Name one area that improved from last meeting.
Name two areas which can be improved for the next meeting.
Be sure to encourage and pray for each member this week.

In several weeks plan to have all group members complete a questionnaire such as this one to evaluate how they feel the group is functioning. Discuss the results openly. Adapt the following questions for your group. For feedback that will contribute to the health of the group remember to be specific in your evaluation questions; be focused on behaviors, not individuals; use wisdom in the timing of the evaluation; base conclusions on the information that is shared; focus on the *what*, not the *why* of actions.

Name _____

Group _____

What has been your most memorable moment in the group? __
_____

What changes would enhance your group experience?_____
_____

How does your group experience improve your life?_____
_____

Please check statements that are true.
__1. Our group members have become good friends.
__2. We have sufficient time on each agenda item.
__3. There is meaningful prayer time in our meeting.
__4. Our group has activities outside our meeting.
__5. We invite others to our group.

__6. Newcomers to the group feel welcomed.
__7. We worked together on a ministry project.
__8. Other comments:

After the evaluation, share results with the group. Remind group members that they have crucial roles—important and different from anyone else's, and that several factors influence the effectiveness of their contributions to the group.

Members may evaluate their participation in the group by responding true or false to these statements.
I . . .
did not participate
argued
expressed my opinion
had to have my way
got my way
could not get interested
gave in
felt hurt
worked it out
helped others work it out
saw new possibilities
was open to what others thought
felt change was not necessary
felt "they" were changing "my" group

Members and leaders might be asked to check the statements which describe how they think the group functioned:
___All members participated.
___Members listened and were open to what others thought.
___Members supported one another.
___We openly worked out differences of opinion.
___We approached the matters on our agenda sincerely.
___We used the time wisely.
___We accomplished our task.

Completing these statements will help you evaluate your leadership role.

I . . .

encouraged others to speak by . . .

played judge when I . . .

was sensitive to someone else by . . .

supported someone by . . .

recalled what was done earlier by saying . . .

dominated when I . . .

suggested a new idea, such as . . .

tried to encourage harmony between . . .

blocked action because . . .

helped move discussion toward a decision by . . .

reminded the members that . . .

tried to solve differences by . . .

gave information and opinions of . . .

played the hero when . . .

clarified a meaning when . . .

summarized information for . . .

Leaders can evaluate group interaction by completing these statements.

Members . . .

raised questions like . . .

doodled or lost interest during . . .

supported someone by . . .

recalled what was done earlier by saying . . .

suggested a new idea, such as . . .

tried to encourage harmony between . . .

blocked action because . . .

helped move discussion toward a decision by . . .

tried to solve differences by . . .

gave information and opinions of . . .

clarified a meaning when . . .

summarized information for . . .

As you completed these statements, you may have discovered that you and your group have problems you were not aware of. Perhaps you and/or others in your group have not accepted your role, or their roles, or perhaps you feel that others have not accepted you. Make a special effort to get to know

40

the other members better and give them the opportunity to know you better. Participate actively in the group, and encourage the other members to do the same.

You might choose to evaluate your group by asking them to discuss how they feel about the:
size of the group
use of meeting time
leadership within the group
materials used for group meetings or projects
relationships with one another
the climate of trust within the group
the amount of freedom to be oneself
the ability to communicate ideas
the ability to communicate feelings
acceptance of each other's faults
concern for each other's struggles
understanding of the purposes and functions of the group
prayer experiences
growth of members within the group
functions, projects, or ministries of the group

Write your responses then share them with the group:

The strong points of our group are:
1.
2.
3.

The problems we need to work through together are:
1.
2.
3.

The group has helped me:
1.
2.
3.

After everyone completes the following form, the leader may want to encourage members to share responses.

SMALL GROUP MEMBER SUMMARY SHEET

MEMBER NAME _____
LEADER _____
PHONE NUMBER _____
GROUP _____
MEETING SCHEDULE _____
(Day, time, and frequency)

GROUP MEMBER'S GIFTS   FUTURE LEADERSHIP POTENTIAL

_____   _____
_____   _____
_____   _____
_____   _____

HOW I PERCEIVE GOALS AND OBJECTIVES OF THE GROUP:

The following would help clarify the intent of this group:

_____
_____
_____
_____

The following are the strong points of the group:

_____
_____
_____
_____

The following areas need improvement:

_____
_____
_____
_____

CIRCLE ONE
I (would, would not) like to lead a similar group in the future.

Review your self-evaluations with a trusted friend who will
be honest with you. Discuss each response; allow them to help
you shape your perceptions. Once you have done this, you will
be able to recognize areas in which you should grow.

CHAPTER 8

Why, When, and How to End a Group

This final phase of group life—ending the team—may be the greatest single influence on how people react to future groups, and how leaders develop as well. Successfully completing this phase is key to participants feeling satisfied, involved, and eager to participate again. During the final phase of the group's life, the leadership should begin to:

•lay groundwork for new groups and new leadership.
•lead the group in understanding and dealing with termination.
•help group members become aware of the psychology of ending a relationship.
•help members focus on accomplishment of the group.
•evaluate and praise accomplishments.
•complete administrative tasks.

Termination of a group requires increased leadership, or a more assertive role by the leader. It technically means moving from a democratic to an authoritative leadership style. The leader must help members deal openly and honestly with the positive, and if appropriate, the negative feelings associated with termination. Remember, all individuals have different, personal feelings about the end of any relationship.

Why and When Groups Terminate

Group leader Neal McBride[1] has identified ten common grounds for group termination, which include:

- *The stated length of time expires.* This is the ideal reason for disbanding groups that began with a clearly defined time span or purpose for existence.
- *The task is accomplished.* This is the primary reason for terminating a group that was created to perform or accomplish a task. Once the task is complete, the group has no purpose for continuing. However, this may be an opportunity for members to become members of another group, or to continue as a group and begin another task or project.
- *The group explodes in conflict.* This reason for ending a group is bad news, and if it happens, it's usually fairly early in a group's life. Try to lead the group to terminate without anger.
- *The group has no covenant or common purpose.* Without a covenant, or agreement on how to proceed, group attendance and behavior can become erratic to the point that members agree that continuing is counterproductive.
- *A conscious decision is made to terminate and remain friends, for whatever reason.* This is a mature choice on the part of group members. Schedule conflicts, members moving out of town, the desire to try something new, or reformation of the group are examples of reasons.
- *Ineffective leadership, or a leader who consistently misses the group's agenda, is another reason.* Though difficult for leaders to admit, they sometimes are in over their heads. Task-, need-, and content-oriented groups are most susceptible to leadership failure. Process-oriented groups tend to be more patient with ineffective leaders.
- *The group divides to form two new groups.* Some churches automatically divide some types of groups when they reach a certain size, and form new groups. This works well in Bible studies and some other situations.
- *The group has poor administration.* Administration problems—such as time, place, frequency, scheduling—can cause members to give up and stop participating. Poor administration generally results from ineffective leadership.
- *There is conflict with other church programs.* Competition among a long list of activities is common in most churches. If people are forced to choose between attending a group or

participating in something else, it's usually indicative of a poor philosophy of ministry—one that sees small groups as just another program option.

- *Members are not compatible.* Termination might well be a logical choice, and one not fueled by conflict. It might be because interests and needs are too dissimilar or there is simply too great a variance in age and experience.

How to Close a Group

Ending a group can be a stressful experience. Whether or not this is the case, it should be done carefully. Friendships built in groups can be among the most meaningful many people have, and there are certain things a leader should take into consideration when closing a group.

- *Don't be reluctant to talk about the end.* Prepare the group for the last meeting before it arrives. Mention the last meeting two or more weeks before it is to occur. Help members to begin to work through the closure process.
- *Use a flexible last meeting format.* The most important thing during the last meeting is making sure people go their separate ways with the greatest amount of comfort and confidence. Allow and urge members to spend some time evaluating their experience together in a positive way.
- *Have fun and encourage one another.* Use an exercise which promotes affirmation. Encourage members to say good things about other group members, or share how the group has been helpful for them. Give everyone the chance to share feelings for the group or individual members.
- *Plan for a future reunion.* If feasible, plan a reunion meeting, so everyone can get together again. Also, let the members know about other opportunities to get involved in groups.
- *Pray together.* Make sure your group takes advantage of what they have built together by making their last prayer time as special as possible.

An Exercise in Terminating a Group

The goals of this exercise are to:
- complete any unfinished business.
- relive and remember the positive group experiences.
- focus on and emphasize the good that group members have received.

• describe and restate members' feelings about the termination of the group.

The theme of the exercise is that although a group may end, the good things its members have given and received, the ways in which they have grown, and the skills learned all continue. Terminating the formal relationship may be sad, but the learning experience can be applied to future group involvement.

Here is a suggested procedure for the group to follow in the exercise:

1. Discuss the topic, "Is there anything that needs to be resolved, discussed, dealt with, or expressed before the group ends?"
2. Discuss these questions: "What have been the most significant experiences of the group? What have I gotten out of being a member of the group? How has being a part of this group facilitated my growth as a person? What skills have I learned from being in this group?" As alternatives to a discussion, group members might collaborate on a painting, collage, or poem describing their experiences.
3. Discuss how you feel about the group winding up its activities and what feelings you want to express about the termination. Personal styles of handling the dissolution of a group may be discussed.
4. Have a group hug if you feel it would be appropriate.

[1]Adapted from *How To Lead Small Groups*. © 1990 by Dr. Neal F. McBride. Used by permission of NavPress, Colorado Springs, Colorado. All rights reserved. For copies call 1-800-366-7788.

Affirmation Activity

For an activity that will encourage affirmation among members, begin a group meeting by asking members to read these Scripture verses to find the common theme:

Proverbs 11:9, 12; 12:6, 16, 24, 27; 22:11

Ecclesiastes 10:12

Romans 14:19

Ephesians 4:29

1 Thessalonians 5:11

Hebrews 10:24-25.

Give members enough slips of paper so that each person has a paper for everyone else in the group. Ask them to write the names of other members and one trait they admire about each member. Then give the papers to the members whose names are on them. Ask each person to read aloud what is written on the paper. This may feel awkward to some who are not accustomed to being showered with affirmation of their good qualities. Encourage them to do the exercise anyway; affirmation is healing and refreshing for the soul!

As each member reads the affirmations, allow time for other members to echo the ideas. You will hear statements such as, "That's right; you really do make people feel at ease." This exercise is quite self-revealing. Members will say things like, "I never knew anyone saw this in me," or "I didn't know I was like this."

In this, or any other group-building exercise, allow plenty of time so members are not rushed. The experience of affirmation should be savored and enjoyed. If any members are absent, fill out slips of paper for them, also; give them the papers later. This exercise should be done only after the group has had a chance to know one another, otherwise they will not know what to affirm. Only statements of affirmation can be given in this exercise. Do not allow any other kind of feedback to be given.

A Communication Exercise

Do members understand the benefits of being part of your group? Have each person list the benefits of participating in a group. You may need to get the exercise started by stating one or two of your reasons for being in a group. Responses may include making new friends, serving in a leadership role, accomplishing a purpose, becoming involved in a ministry or project, making a difference in the world. Don't be afraid to listen to and deal with any negative comments.

After members have had time to write their reasons, list all the reasons on a flipchart, chalkboard, or large sheet of paper. Ask several volunteers to share their most positive group experience. Ask, *What made it so special?*

This exercise will have several benefits. Members will understand more about their participation in and benefits from the group. As the leader, you will gain an appreciation of members expectations. It will give you the opportunity to share your vision for the group. Additionally, group members can become aware of the purpose of the group, and become unified in meeting that purpose.

Group Member's Prayer

At an appropriate time, distribute copies of the following group member's prayer. During prayer time, use the prayer to enhance group participation.

Father help me:
•prepare before my group meeting.
•come with an expectant attitude.
•be willing to learn from others.
•really listen to others in the group.
• give my full attention to the discussion.
• be sensitive to how others feel about the things they are talking about.
• not monopolize the group, or speak too little.

- help when a problem arises.
- be honest about myself and my thinking and speak the truth in love.
- keep the group on its main purpose.
- look for applications for my own thinking and action.
- encourage people and pray for others in their various ministries from week to week.
- accept encouragement from others in the group.
- carry out my ministry.

Sharing Questions

One way to build relationships within a group is by using questions that will help members share with one another. Group leader Roberta Hestenes[1] gives suggestions to help you develop questions that will accomplish group building.

- Think about where your group is now. Do members need most to think about their own or the group's past, present, or future? Does the focus need to be affirmation or accountability? After deciding on the focus of the question, write questions which asks for information or factual material in the area of focus. Here are some examples:

  Past: When is the first time you remember encouraging someone and how did you feel about that?

  Present: What is a good thing happening in your life right now and what makes it good?

  Future: What is one change you would like to make in your life in the next two years and why?

  Affirmation: What is one thing you appreciate about one other member of this group and why?

  Accountability: What is one responsibility you have to fulfill this next week and how do you feel about that?

- Questions should call for information not readily available to other group members such as: What is a typical Tuesday like for you? Describe your day briefly beginning with when you get up and when you go to bed. What do you like most and like least in your day?

- Ask questions which can be answered briefly (in three minutes or less) if the group is new or wants to spend a limited amount of time on sharing. Remember that three minutes per person, with 10 people, will take at least 30 minutes.

Good questions will:
- be understandable without further explanation. Do not include words or concepts that need to be defined.
- not require people to give more information about themselves than they feel comfortable doing. (Do not ask, "What is your worst fault?")
- be easily answered by every member of the group. Questions such as "Where did you attend college?" might not be appropriate in most situations.
- be beneficial to other group members as they listen. Some responses might be inappropriate or of no interest to others.
- help the group members to know each other better, enabling them to understand and love each other.
- not call for simple yes/no responses. Also, avoid asking for the best and worst, but rather ask for a good and a not-so-good.
- have enough variety in response so that all members are not saying the same thing. For example, a good question is, "Who is one important person in your life and why?"
- ask for personal sharing of the self, not for opinions on issues.
- be related to the purpose or focus of the group rather than be a tacked-on extra.

Hestenes suggest these "ground rules" for the use of sharing questions in a group:
- Allow people to pass if they are not ready to respond. Do check back with them at the end of the sharing time to see if they wish to share now. Don't force them to share.
- Mix questions which call for negative and positive sharing. Don't always ask people to share problems or always to share victories. Mix them up.
- Don't ask follow-up questions after people share unless you intend for only a few to speak. Affirm nonverbally or briefly what has been shared and move on to the next person.
- Usually you ask someone to begin sharing and then go in a circle from there. Begin yourself only if no one else could go first comfortably; if you do begin, be brief.
- Watch the time. If the first one or two members speak at length, intervene by saying, "Let's share briefly so all may have a chance to speak."

Conversational Prayer

One way to build group unity is by using conversational prayer. Following are some suggested guidelines to share with your group if you plan to use conversational prayer.

- Be brief. Pray only one or two sentences at a time.
- Use everyday language. Pray in language an eight-year-old could understand.
- Allow for silence.
- Pray randomly, not in a circle.
- Give permission for participants not to pray. It is appropriate for as many as wish to voice prayers. If the group is large it is okay for several members to pray, with the leader closing.
- Limit time for prayer requests. Instead of listing requests then praying, encourage members to pray their requests.
- Pray with and for one another.
- The leader designates a person to open (prearranged). The leader closes.

Following are three examples of conversational prayers:

- Example 1: John's wife Mary is in the hospital.

1st person: Father, we lift Mary up to You for healing.

2nd person: Father, strengthen John and the children during this difficult period.

3rd person: Lord, provide for the family's financial needs during Mary's hospitalization.

4th person: God, we pray safe travel for Mary's mother.

5th person/leader: Thank you Father for letting us come to You with all our needs, and for hearing and answering. In Your Son's holy and precious name we pray. Amen.

- Example 2: Praying for individual concerns.

1st person: Father, watch over my son during his senior finals.

2nd person: Heavenly father, lift up my aunt Susan as she is tested for cancer.

3rd person: Dear God, heal the Smith family.

4th person: Father, I praise You for my son's recovery from hepatitis.

5th person/leader: Lord, I pray for guidance in my decision on a job change, and that Your will be done. In Jesus' name, Amen.

• Example 3: Praying for ministry needs to others

1st person: Father, we have just become aware of the number of homeless families living in our neighborhood.

2nd person: Lord, I confess that I've not been as concerned as I should have been about their physical needs. I thank You that You led me to these other people who also have become aware of this need.

3rd person: Dear God, as we begin our food pantry, I ask that You will bless the ministry, and that You will help members of our church realize the blessings they will receive as they take part in this ministry.

4th person: Father, I praise You already for the victories that will come as we serve others in Your name.

5th person/leader: Lord, I pray for guidance for our group as we begin this new ministry. In Jesus' name, Amen.

What Would You Do if . . .

Possible solutions to the situations described on pages 20-21. What would you do if . . .

• more than half the group members are late?

Begin on time. When it is appropriate without embarrassing the late-comers, review the agreed start and stop times. Discuss the reasons for tardiness; it could be you need to change the time or day you meet.

• two group members are carrying on a private conversation during the meeting?

If the problem is annoying to the entire group, ask one of the talkers a question. If the problem continues, meet with them after the meeting and address the issue. Ask yourself if the two have enough responsibilities within the group. If your group members are adults, remember that fact when you approach this problem. Do not make group members feel you are treating them like children.

• members cannot come to a consensus?

Have all members had an opportunity to voice their views? Is this an important decision? In the past, have group members been allowed to make decisions? If the answers to these questions are "yes," then take time as a group to list on a flip chart the alternatives along with the advantages and disadvantages, then draw a conclusion.

• you don't have enough time to complete the priority items on your agenda?

If you have not been assigning time limits by each agenda item, start now. If appropriate, assign certain items to a subgroup. With group consent, extend your meeting time.

• you observe leadership qualities in a group member?

Meet with the person and share your observations on their leadership skills. If appropriate, ask them to be a co-leader with you. Ask if you can give this person's name to other organizations or groups that may be looking for leaders.

• a member frequently misses meetings?

If you as the leader, or another person in the group, contact all members on a regular basis, you will know why someone is absent before the fact. If you have not been in contact, call the member and ask why they have missed. Show genuine concern, and stress the value of the member to the group.

• two or more members begin to argue?

Tactfully interrupt. Give other group members the opportunity to comment. If necessary, meet with the two members after the meeting to make sure feelings are calm and both feel they have been heard.

• you are having a bad day and it's time for your meeting?

Be honest by admitting your situation. It's okay for members of your group to know you are human. This is a great opportunity to have a member with leadership potential fill in for you. Allow the group to pray for your needs and the needs of others.

[1]Adapted from Hestenses, Roberta, *Using the Bible in Groups.* © 1983 Roberta Hestenes. Used by permission of Westminster/John Knox Press.

Group Study Guide

Note: Since this book is about group-building skills, the group study guide is especially important. Use the study time not only to teach the book, but also to demonstrate group-building skills. The plan below is for a 2 ½ hour study. An alternate one hour plan is also given.

Preparation:
1. Read the book carefully, completing all personal learning activities. Read this study guide, making notes of your own plans for teaching.
2. Secure books for all participants; encourage them to read the book before the study.
3. Secure any materials you plan to use during the study.
4. As you prepare, pray for yourself as a leader, and for those who will participate.

Introductory activity (15 minutes)
Ask participants to discover five facts about one other person, then introduce that friend to the group. If the group is large, limit introduction time to only one fact about each participant.

As they move through this study, suggest that participants identify their relationship to one particular group. They may be the leader or facilitator of an existing group, a leader or facilitator of a group that is about to begin, or the member of a group.

Book study (one hour)
Briefly review the functions and mechanics of a group from chapter 1. Ask members to describe the primary function of the group they are a part of, then evaluate how well the group accomplishes its functions. Ask participants to suggest reasons groups are formed. Do the Communication Exercise (p. 48).

On a chalkboard or large sheet of paper, list the five characteristics of a group leader that are given in chapter 2. Working with one other person, participants will discuss why each of these characteristics is important for a group leader. Ask participants to complete the Personal Point of View exercises.

Arrange participants in four small groups. Assign one of the leadership styles described in chapter 3 to each group. Groups will role play a leader who has this leadership style. Give groups five to ten minutes to prepare. The presentations should be a fun learning experience.

After the presentations, ask each group to discuss possible solutions for two of the case studies (pp. 20-21) then report to the large group. Be prepared to give suggestions from page 52, but do not refer to these until after the group report.

Break (15 minutes)

Book study continued (one hour)

Begin this part of the study by describing and giving examples of conversation prayer (see pp. 50-51). If members feel comfortable doing so, have a time of conversation prayer.

On four sheets of paper, write the four personality types described on page 23. Ask members to think of contributions each of these personalities make to the group. Also, ask them to think of potential problems this personality may encounter. Ask, when group members use their spiritual gifts, how do they help the group accomplish its purpose?

Ask participants to look at the suggestions for developing sharing questions (p. 49), then work with one other person to think of some questions they could use at their next group meeting.

Draw a line down the center of a large sheet of paper. Ask participants to list healthy and unhealthy characteristics of a group in the columns. As they are given, ask members to think of steps that could be taken to help the unhealthy group. Participants can refer to information in chapter 5.

Lead participants in a review of the list of pitfalls (pp. 34-35) a group may encounter. As they review the list, ask members to identify problems their group has encountered, or potential problems. Encourage them to discuss possible solutions.

Ask participants to suggest reasons evaluation is an important step in group building. Review the evaluations in chapter 7, then ask participants to work with one other person to develop an evaluation they can use in the next meeting of their group.

Briefly discuss some of the reasons a group may end, and ways to terminate a group. Allow participants to give suggestions and share experiences they have had.

Conclusion (15 minutes)

Ask participants to review personal benefits of this study. Encourage them to be specific, and name ways this study will help them be a better leader, facilitator, or member of their group. Ask participants to read responsively the Group Member's Prayer (pp. 50-51).

For a one hour study, encourage participants to read the book and complete the Personal Point of View exercises. Spend the first ten minutes in the introductory activity; overview each chapter of the book during the next 45 minutes. Close with the responsive reading of the Group Member's Prayer.

Church Study Course

Group Building Skills is course number 03-351 in the subject area: Christian Growth and Service. Credit for the course may be obtained in two ways: (1) conference or class—read the book and participate in a 2½-hour study; (2) individual study—read the book, do the personal learning activities, and have a church leader check written work.

Request credit on form 725 Church Study Course Enrollment/Credit Request (rev.) available from the Church Study Course Awards Office, 127 Ninth Avenue North, Nashville, TN 37234.

Complete details about the Church Study Course system, courses available, and diplomas offered is in the Church Study Course Catalog available form the Church Study Course Awards Office.

Group Building Skills is one of five books in the *Leadership Skills for Women* series. These books are written *by* women *for* women as each exercises her God-given gifts to advance His kingdom.

OTHER BOOKS IN THE
Leadership Skills for Women series

Name _____

Address: _____

City: _____ST___ ZIP _____

Daytime phone # _____

Code #	Title	Qty.	Cost	Total
W923125	*With A Servant Heart*		$3.95	
N933105	*Relationship Skills*		$5.95	
N943116	*Time Management Skills*		$5.95	
N943117	*Conflict Management Skills*		$5.95	
N943115	*Communication Skills*		$5.95	
N933107	*Group Building Skills*		$5.95	

**Alabama Sales Tax	*Shipping & Handling		
8% Birmingham	0- $15.00 $2.50	Subtotal	
5% Jefferson County	$15.01-$50.00 $3.25	**AL customers add tax	
6% Shelby County	$50.01-$100.00 $4.00	*Shipping & Handling	
4% Other Alabama	$100.01-& up $5.00	TOTAL ENCLOSED	

Send to:
New Hope
P. O. Box 12065
Birmingham, AL
35202-2065

(205) 991-4933

Order will arrive in four to six weeks.

PAYMENT MUST ACCOMPANY ORDER
☐ Check ☐ VISA ☐ MasterCard
PLEASE DO NOT SEND CASH

CARD NUMBER

EXPIRATION DATE

4 DIGIT BANK CODE
(MasterCard Only)

Authorizing Signature

M94NHLDS